American Habitats

Forest Animals

Connor Dayton

PowerKiDS press
New York

Published in 2009 by The Rosen Publishing Group, Inc.
29 East 21st Street, New York, NY 10010

First Edition

Editor: Nicole Pristash
Book Design: Greg Tucker
Photo Researcher: Jessica Gerweck

Photo Credits: Cover, back cover, pp. 7, 11, 17 Shutterstock.com; p. 5 © www.istockphoto.com/Mark Hatfield; p. 9 © www.istockphoto.com; p. 13 © Buddy Mays/Getty Images; p. 15 © Norbert Rosing/Getty Images; p. 19 © Chris Johns/Getty Images; p. 21 © Vicom/Peter Arnold, Inc.

Library of Congress Cataloging-in-Publication Data

Dayton, Connor.
Forest animals / Connor Dayton. — 1st ed.
p. cm. — (American habitats)
Includes index.
ISBN 978-1-4358-2764-6 (library binding) — ISBN 978-1-4358-3193-3 (pbk.)
ISBN 978-1-4358-3199-5 (6-pack)
1. Forest animals—Juvenile literature. I. Title.
QL112.D39 2009
591.73—dc22
2008034413

Manufactured in the United States of America

Contents

America's Forest Animals

A forest is one of the many **habitats** that can be found in the United States. If you walked through a **temperate** forest, you might see porcupines, gray squirrels, or **cardinals**. You might even see a black bear, too! A temperate forest is warm for part of the year and cold during the other part.

A **tropical** rain forest is warm and wet year-round. On a walk through a rain forest, you might see bright butterflies and a red bird called the 'i'iwi. Let's take a look at these two forest habitats and the animals that live in them.

Raccoons, like the one shown here, have gray or brown fur and a black mask around their eyes. Raccoons are some of the most common forest animals.

Changing Seasons

In the United States, temperate forests are found from southern New England to the Midwest. The **precipitation** in temperate forests is even throughout the year, but the **temperature** changes with each season. Winters are cold and summers are warm. Leafy trees, such as the oak and the maple, lose their leaves when the weather cools in the fall. These trees bud new leaves in the spring.

Temperate forests grow other plants, such as wild berries, flowers, and mosses. These plants are food for the animals that call the temperate forest home.

Habitat Facts

Some temperate forests have both leafy trees and coniferous trees. Coniferous trees, such as pine and spruce trees, keep their needlelike leaves year-round. These trees are also called evergreens.

Temperate forests, like this one, can be very dense. In a dense forest, there are a lot of trees, and light has a hard time shining through.

Forest Mammals

Many **mammals** live in temperate forests. Mammals have fur that keeps them warm. The fur's colors help the mammals mix in with the colors of the forest. Some of the mammals that live in temperate forests are white-tailed deer, coyotes, red foxes, and raccoons.

The black bear is another type of mammal found in a temperate forest. Black bears can be up to 6 feet (2 m) long and weigh 600 pounds (272 kg). They eat plants, fish, dead animals, and even trash. Campers need to store their food and trash carefully to make sure black bears stay away!

Animal Facts

Black bears have sharp claws on their paws. Their claws allow them to climb trees in order to stay safe. Black bears also climb trees to sleep and to eat nuts and fruit.

Black bears can see in color, and they have sharp eyesight close-up. Black bears can also see objects that are more than 200 yards (183 m) away.

Hunters in the Sky

As you walk through a temperate forest, look up at the birds. Robins and cardinals live in nests in the trees. These birds fly down from their nests to eat berries, bugs, and worms. Robins and cardinals also bring food back to their nests for their babies to eat.

Great horned owls are birds of **prey**. They use their sharp hearing and eyesight to hunt in a temperate forest at night. The great horned owl's special feathers let it fly quietly so it can sneak up on its prey. These owls hunt mice, squirrels, rabbits, and small birds.

The great horned owl begins its hunt by sitting on a tree branch and looking for its prey. Then, the owl dives to the ground to catch it.

Bugs of the Forest

If you get down on the ground, you will see some of the smallest animals of a temperate forest. Insects, or bugs, live in the ground, under rocks, and in rotting logs. Moths, ants, and ladybugs are some of the insects that you may spot.

Black widow spiders can be found living near logs in a temperate forest. Female black widows have a red marking on their bodies. They eat small insects that they trap in their webs using their **venomous** bites. Be careful if you see a female black widow because its bite can hurt you and make you sick.

Animal Facts

Female black widow spiders generally do not cause death when they bite someone. This is because they have only a small amount of venom in their bites.

This is a female black widow spider. Female black widows are around 1 ½ inches (4 cm) long, and they weigh only .04 ounces (1 g).

A Croak and a Hiss

If you walk near a pond in a temperate forest, you may see fish and **amphibians**. Fish, such as the brook trout, live in rivers that run throughout temperate forests.

You might hear a bullfrog's loud croak before you see the bullfrog. These amphibians live among plants by the water. Bullfrogs use quick flicks of their tongues to catch and eat insects that come their way.

You may also spot some **reptiles** as you walk through a temperate forest. If you look along the ground, you might catch a garter snake or a black rat snake crossing your path.

When garter snakes come together to make babies, they often wrap around each other in a large group like this. This is called a mating ball.

Hawaiian Forests

A tropical rain forest is a type of forest that gets a lot of rain and stays around the same temperature all year long. Hawaii is the only U.S. state that has a tropical rain forest. Hawaii's rain forests have many different plants, such as fruit trees, bushes, and grasses.

With warm weather and so many plants, Hawaii is home to lots of animals. Some of these animals are native to the Hawaiian islands. Other animals were brought to Hawaii by people over time. Let's take a closer look at both the native and the nonnative Hawaiian animals.

This is a rain forest on Hawaii's Big Island. In Hawaii, rain forests are in places that are between 1,350 and 6,300 feet (411–1,920 m) high.

Hawaiian Natives

As you walk through a Hawaiian rain forest, you will see many butterflies. However, the Kamehameha butterfly is one of the few butterflies that are native to Hawaii. This reddish orange butterfly is sometimes mixed up with the more common, nonnative monarch butterfly.

The 'i'iwi, or Hawaiian honeycreeper, will be easy to spot. It is a bright red bird with a curved bill. The 'i'iwi generally lives on the Big Island and the island of Kauai, but some also live on the islands of Molokai and Oahu. The 'i'iwi has a squeaky call that sounds like balloons rubbing together.

This 'i'iwi's curved bill, shown here, helps the 'i'iwi drink nectar. Nectar is sweet matter found in flowers.

A New Home in Hawaii

Many nonnative animals live in Hawaii, too. Most of the butterflies that fly around Hawaii were brought there, but they have made Hawaii their home. The monarch butterfly has settled in and become one of the most common butterflies in Hawaii.

The coqui frog is a native of Puerto Rico. Coqui frogs were brought to Hawaii by mistake, and they have spread throughout Hawaii's rain forests. This tiny frog's name comes from its croak, which sounds like "ko-KEE." Some people think the coqui is cute, but others consider it a pest whose loud calls keep them up at night!

Coqui frogs are very tiny frogs. They are only around 1 inch (2.5 cm) long!

Conservation

Many animals in the United States make temperate forests and tropical rain forests their homes. The forest habitat needs to be kept safe for the wildlife inside it. Doing so is called conservation. There are things you can do to help conserve forests.

Keeping bad gases out of the air keeps plants and animals from dying. Keeping forests clean gives plants and animals a nice, safe home to live in. To learn more about conservation, you can ask your teacher or read about it at school. Taking care of America's forests will allow people and animals to continue enjoying them.